Regions of America

The South

Francie Dolan

NorwoodHouse Press

Cataloging-in-Publication Data

Names: Dolan, Francie.
Title: The South / Francie Dolan.
Description: Buffalo, NY : Norwood House Press, 2027. | Series: Regions of America | Includes glossary and index.
Identifiers: ISBN 9781978581227 (pbk.) | ISBN 9781978581234 (library bound) | ISBN 9781978581241 (ebook)
Subjects: LCSH: Southern States--Juvenile literature.
Classification: LCC F209.3 D65 2027 | DDC 975--dc23

Published in 2027 by
Norwood House Press
2544 Clinton Street
Buffalo, NY 14224

Designer: Rhea Magaro
Editor: Tricia Hoffman

Photo credits: Cover, p. 1 Kevin Ruck/Shutterstock.com; p. 5 Just dance/Shutterstock.com; p. 6 Wirestock Creators/Shutterstock.com; p. 7 mariakray/Shutterstock.com; p. 8 art4you1/Shutterstock.com; p. 10 casa.da.photo/Shutterstock.com; p. 11 MarkVanDykePhotography/Shutterstock.com; p. 12 Library of Congress; p. 13 EWY Media/Shutterstock.com; p. 14 Everett Collection; p. 15 Wikipedia; p. 17 Chin Ting Chan/Shutterstock.com; p. 18 HannaChu/Shutterstock.com; p. 21 Felix Mizioznikov/Shutterstock.com; p. 21 Zack Frank/Shutterstock.com;

Printed in the United States of America

CPSIA compliance information: Batch #CSNHP27: For further information contact Norwood House Press at 1-800-237-9932.

TABLE OF CONTENTS

WHERE IS THE SOUTH?

The South is a **region** of the United States.

It has 10 states.

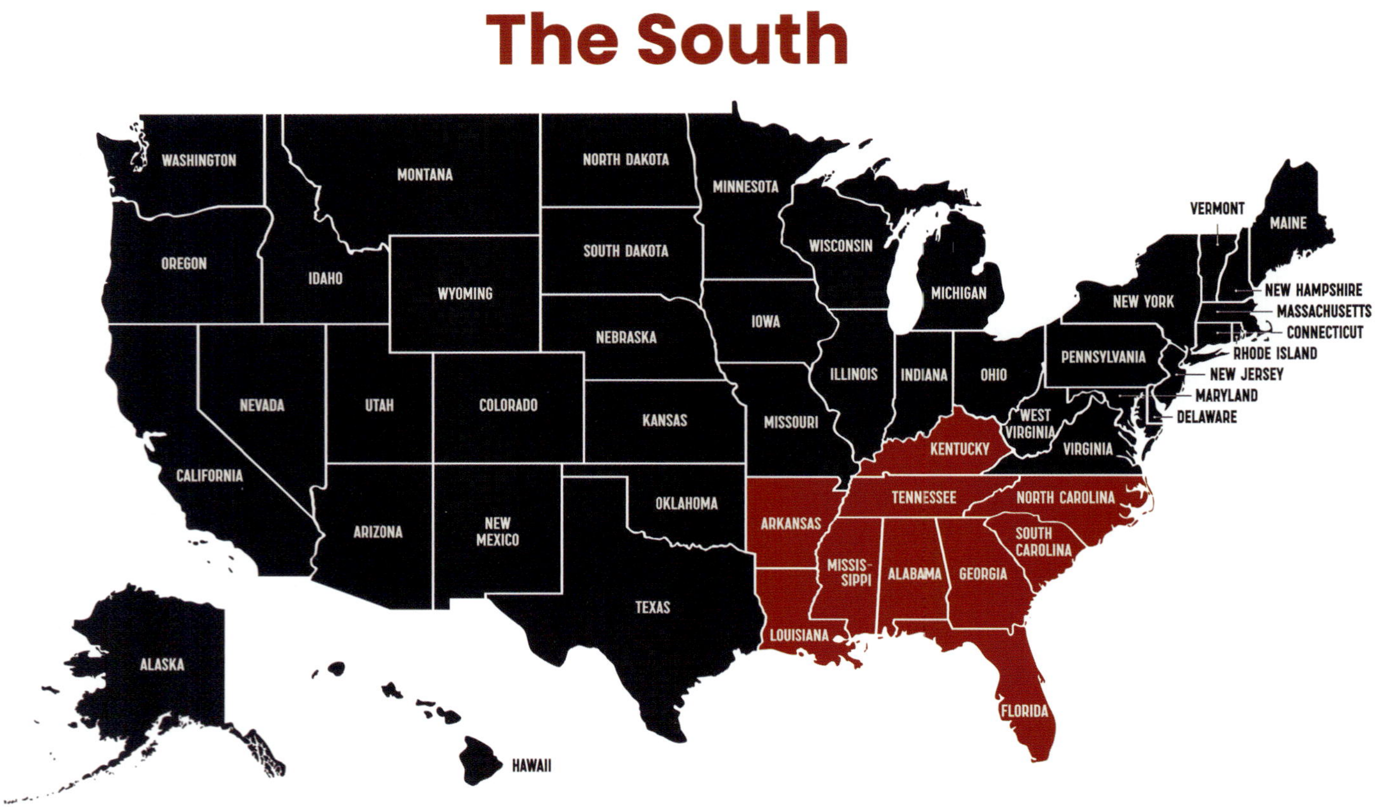

THE LAND

The South is in the southeastern part of the country. Most of its states lie east of the Mississippi River.

Most of the South is **subtropical**. It rarely gets cold enough for snow to fall.

Some states border the Atlantic Ocean. Others border the Gulf of America. Low **coastal** plains cover much of the land. This tidewater region has **marshes**, rivers, swamps, and **bayous**. They rise and fall with ocean tides.

The soil is **fertile**. Southern farms grow cotton, rice, peanuts, and other crops.

The Appalachian Mountains run through part of the South. Their tops are rounded. They are covered with trees. They formed hundreds of millions of years ago.

THE PEOPLE

Indigenous people once lived across the region. Some tribes were the Cherokee and Seminole.

Parts of the South were once claimed by France and Spain. Today, you can eat French food in Louisiana. You can visit old Spanish forts in Florida.

More than 150 years ago, Black people from Africa were forced to come to the South to work. After **slavery** became against the law, many remained.

The Gullah people live in Georgia, South Carolina, and other places in the South. Their language, food, and music come from Africa.

THINGS TO SEE AND DO

In Kentucky, you can go underground to explore Mammoth Cave. It is the world's longest known cave system.

In Atlanta, Georgia, you can see the house where Martin Luther King, Jr. was born. The great **Civil Rights** leader spent most of his life in the city.

In Florida, you can ride an **airboat** through the Everglades. This vast, watery wilderness is called a "river of grass." You may see manatees, panthers, and many other animals. It's the only place in the world where alligators and crocodiles live together.

GLOSSARY

airboat (AIR-boht): a shallow boat driven by an airplane propeller

bayous (BYE-ooz): streams that run slowly through swamps and that connect to a lake or river

Civil Rights (SIV-uhl rites): related to a period from 1954 to 1968 when Black people in America fought to gain equal rights under the law

coastal (KOH-stuhl): near the ocean

fertile (FUR-tuhl): good for growing; rich and full of nutrients

Indigenous (in-DI-juh-nuhs): the earliest known people to live in a place

marshes (MAHR-shiz): areas of wet, muddy land

region (REE-juhn): an area or territory; part of a country

slavery (SLAY-vur-ee): a system in which people are kidnapped, kept against their will, and made to work without pay or rights; slavery of Black people was legal in the United States before the Civil War

subtropical (suhb-TRAH-pi-kuhl): next to tropical areas that are close to Earth's equator; often hot and rainy

THINKING QUESTIONS

1. Name three states in the South.

2. Describe a tidewater region.

3. Name one Native American tribe from the South.

4. What can you see in Atlanta, Georgia?

5. What are the Everglades?

INDEX

ABOUT THE AUTHOR

Francie Dolan is a writer from Seattle, Washington. She loves American history and trivia. It is her goal to travel to all 50 states, visit their capital cities, and eat a special food from each place.